W9-DGO-672

Franklin School
Summit Public Schools

WOMEN IN STEM

WOMEN IN
CONSERVATION

by Carol Hand

Content Consultant
Claudia A. Radel, PhD
Associate Professor, Human Geography
Utah State University

Core Library

An Imprint of Abdo Publishing
abdopublishing.com

abdopublishing.com

Published by Abdo Publishing, a division of ABDO, PO Box 398166, Minneapolis, Minnesota 55439. Copyright © 2017 by Abdo Consulting Group, Inc. International copyrights reserved in all countries. No part of this book may be reproduced in any form without written permission from the publisher. Core Library™ is a trademark and logo of Abdo Publishing.

Printed in the United States of America, North Mankato, Minnesota
032016
092016

THIS BOOK CONTAINS
RECYCLED MATERIALS

Cover Photo: Jeff Rotman/Science Source
Interior Photos: Jeff Rotman/Science Source, 1; Kennan Ward/Corbis, 4; AP Images, 8, 43; Heng Sinith/AP Images, 10; Kevin Fleming/Corbis, 12; Astrid Stawiarz/Getty Images, 17; Jens Lambert Photography/iStockphoto, 18; Pete Oxford/Minden Pictures/Corbis, 20; Bettmann/Corbis, 23; US Navy, 26; Ammit Jack/Shutterstock Images, 28, 45; Bjorn Sigurdson/AP Images, 31; M-Sat Ltd/Science Source, 33; Peter Bennett/Science Source, 34; Stanley Breeden & Belinda Wright/National Geographic/Getty Images, 37; Themba Hadebe/AP Images, 40

Editor: Arnold Ringstad
Series Designer: Laura Polzin

Cataloging-in-Publication Data
Names: Hand, Carol, author.
Title: Women in conservation / by Carol Hand.
Description: Minneapolis, MN : Abdo Publishing, [2017] | Series: Women in
   STEM | Includes bibliographical references and index.
Identifiers: LCCN 2015960508 | ISBN 9781680782653 (lib. bdg.) |
   ISBN 9781680776768 (ebook)
Subjects: LCSH: Women environmentalists--Juvenile literature. | Women
   conservationists--Juvenile literature. | Women naturalists--Juvenile literature.
Classification: DDC 333.7--dc23
LC record available at http://lccn.loc.gov/2015960508

CONTENTS

CHAPTER ONE

LEADING THE WAY

Jane Goodall arrived at Gombe Stream in the summer of 1960. This nature reserve is in Tanzania, a country in East Africa. She was 26 years old. Goodall soon became the world's top expert on the chimpanzees of Gombe. She tracked the apes. She was interested in their social lives. She watched how they interacted. Her work changed the

Goodall has been working to protect chimpanzees for decades.

field of ethology. This is the study of animal behavior. Goodall became a powerful defender of chimpanzees.

Jane Goodall and STEM

Goodall's work blazed a path for women in STEM careers. STEM stands for science, technology, engineering, and mathematics. Most people expect STEM careers to involve things such as computers, rockets, or robots. Many of these careers do. Even Goodall uses technology. But her STEM career began with simple handwritten notes.

Goodall did not set out to open a path for women. She was only following her dream. She was determined to study animals in Africa. She did

Inspiring Followers

Jane Goodall's work has inspired many women. Two famous ones also worked with apes. Like Goodall, they lived in the wilderness. Dian Fossey studied mountain gorillas in the African country of Rwanda. She founded the Karisoke Research Center. Dr. Biruté Galdikas studied orangutans on the Asian island of Borneo. She has received many awards for her work.

not let anything stop her. Goodall convinced people that chimps were not just research subjects. They were individuals with personalities. They had thoughts and emotions. Before Goodall's work, scientists did not believe this. Now they do.

A Different Kind of Pioneer

Another pioneer lived a very different life. Rachel Carson was a marine biologist. She worked for the US Fish and Wildlife Service in the 1940s. She wrote prize-winning books about oceans. Then she became aware of dangerous pesticides. She recognized they posed threats to wildlife.

IN THE REAL WORLD

Attacking a Female Scientist

Pesticide companies called Rachel Carson a "radical." They said she was a "sentimental nature lover" who misused science. Magazines such as *Time* and *Life* said she "looked like more of a teacher or a stay-at-home mother." They ignored her scientific training. Many people now call Carson the mother of the environmental movement. But some still condemn her work.

Carson took her conservation message to the US Senate in 1963.

She spent years researching their effects. In 1962 she published her book *Silent Spring*. *Silent Spring* warned people of the risks of certain pesticides. The companies that made these chemicals criticized her.

Carson battled people in the chemical industry and the government. The attacks did not stop her. She spoke before Congress. She asked for new rules to protect the environment. The government banned a pesticide called DDT. Carson's *Silent Spring* helped inspire an environmental movement.

Women, STEM, and Conservation

Conservation and environmental studies form one STEM field. Scientists in this field do many things. They preserve animal habitats. They collect information about wildlife. They carry out plans to protect nature. Many write about environmental problems. Others measure or repair damage to ecosystems. They clean up polluted areas.

Conservation jobs are exciting. People in conservation can make a real difference in the world. These workers are more important every year. Human populations spread out and take over natural habitats. Animals lose their homes. People kill animals for money or products, such as ivory from elephants. The animals may become endangered. They may even go extinct. Conservationists try to prevent this. They work hard and get dirty. They sometimes even face danger.

A conservation worker in Cambodia holds a rescued sun bear.

Women in these fields love nature. They want to protect it. But women have only approximately 28 percent of US environmental science jobs. The world needs many more of today's girls to become tomorrow's conservation leaders.

Jane Goodall wrote about how her approach to research differed from the accepted practices of the time:

> *I had not been to college and there were many things about animal behavior that I did not know. I had not been taught, for example, that it was wrong to give names to my study subjects—it would have been more scientific to give them numbers. I was dumbfounded by this practice. . . . I did not think of the chimps as "study subjects" but as individuals, each with his or her own personality. I was learning from them, not only about them. . . . I was also reprimanded . . . for ascribing personalities to the different chimpanzees—as though I had made up the vivid and unique characteristics of the various members of the . . . community! Only humans have personalities, I was told. Nor should I have been talking about the chimpanzee mind— only humans, said the scientists, were capable of rational thought.*

> Source: Dale Peterson. *Jane Goodall: The Woman Who Redefined Man.* New York: Mariner Books, 2008. Print. 276–277.

What's the Big Idea?

Describe how Goodall says scientists felt about her chimpanzees. Do you think Goodall agrees with their attitudes? How would you describe her attitude toward the chimps?

US WOMEN ENVIRONMENTALISTS

Amerian women have long fought for animal rights. They have also worked to help the environment. They did this throughout the 1800s and early 1900s. Rosalie Edge founded the first preserve for birds of prey. This was the Hawk Mountain Sanctuary in the Appalachian Mountains. Marjory Stoneman Douglas protected the Everglades in Florida. Margaret "Mardy" Murie fought to

Marjory Stoneman Douglas in the Florida Everglades

Saving the Birds

Conservation is not a new idea. In the late 1800s, humans hunted five million birds every year. They used the birds to make feather hats. Hunters killed many types of birds. They included snowy egrets, great blue herons, and even songbirds. Women conservationists rallied to save the birds. They started protests. They pledged not to wear bird feathers. In 1918 the US government passed the Migratory Bird Treaty Act. The law made it illegal to capture or kill certain types of birds. This stopped the use of bird feathers in hats. The groups who organized the protests became the National Audubon Society.

preserve Alaska's wilderness.

Conservation Scientists

Few women had the opportunity to leave home before the mid-1900s. Most were unable to have adventures and write about wild nature. Women such as Jane Goodall and Rachel Carson showed that women can be conservationists. Modern women still fight for conservation. Some are environmental scientists.

Dr. Gretchen Daily is a professor at Stanford University. She works to conserve biodiversity. This is the variety of living things that exist in an area. Dr. Jane Lubchenco is a professor at Oregon State University. She has worked to restore ocean fisheries and coastal areas. She also teaches about climate change. "The oceans and other ecosystems are in very serious trouble," Lubchenco says, "and we need to think about, treat, and value them differently."

Conservation Activists

Activists are citizens who work for change. In May 2015, activist Chiara D'Angelo chained herself to a ship. The ship was located in Bellingham Bay, Washington. Royal Dutch Shell, the ship's owner, planned to drill for oil

IN THE REAL WORLD

Carol Ruckdeschel

Carol Ruckdeschel lives on Cumberland Island, Georgia. For decades, she has fought against developers who want to build on the island. Ruckdeschel especially wants to save Cumberland's sea turtles. She swims and dives with them off the shore. She has written scientific papers. She has talked with politicians about protecting Cumberland and its turtles.

off the Alaska coast. D'Angelo opposed the drilling and wanted to block it from happening. Her action gained public attention. Shell later stopped Arctic oil exploration. Activism helped change the company's plans. Most environmental activism is not so exciting. It is hard work that requires persistence. But these efforts can lead to important change.

Winona LaDuke is a Native American. She has founded several projects to help Native Americans and the environments in which they live. These include efforts to keep Native American lands clean and healthy.

Majora Carter is from the South Bronx in New York City. Carter works to reduce poverty and crime rates through environmental work. Her projects include the creation of green spaces. These are areas in the inner city with trees and other plants. They help make cities more attractive to residents and local businesses.

Majora Carter speaks at an event in 2009.

The fracking process has become controversial due to its effects on the environment.

Sandra Steingraber studies how chemicals in the environment affect human health. She is most concerned with hydraulic fracturing, or fracking. In this process, drillers inject water containing toxic chemicals into the ground. This makes it easier to pump out oil and natural gas. Critics worry that the leftover chemicals can enter drinking water sources. Steingraber writes and speaks about this danger. She has even been arrested because of her protests. This happened when she blocked the driveway of a natural gas company.

Over the years, the types of environmental issues in the headlines have changed. Women have continued to contribute to conservation efforts. The future will bring new challenges. Female conservationists will continue fighting for the environment.

EXPLORE ONLINE

Chapter Two discusses the work of US women scientists and activists in conservation. The website below includes more information about these and other well-known conservationists. As you know, every source is different. How do the chapter and the website present information differently? What new information did you learn from the website?

Women Conservationists, Always Ahead of the Curve
mycorelibrary.com/women-in-conservation

CHAPTER THREE

WOMEN SAVING THE OCEANS

Pollution, climate change, and overfishing are harming the oceans. Animals and plants are beginning to go extinct. Scientists expect more to die. To save oceans, we must understand them. Many women are becoming marine biologists and oceanographers.

A diver works to conserve a coral reef off the coast of Fiji.

Sylvia Earle, Ocean Explorer

Dr. Sylvia Earle has spent nearly a year of her life in the oceans. In 1970 she led an all-female crew in spending two weeks in a tiny habitat 50 feet (15 m) underwater. The habitat was called Tektite II. The Tektite mission made Earle famous. She began giving speeches on undersea research. She wrote articles and books and made films to teach people about the oceans.

Earle has studied oceans around the world. In 1979 she descended to 1,250 feet (381 m) below the surface off the Hawaii coast in a submersible. When she reached the sea floor, she left the

The Shark Lady

Eugenie Clark was called the "Shark Lady." This marine biologist died in 2015 at age 92. Clark pioneered underwater research using scuba gear and submersibles. She wrote books and taught college courses. She educated the public about ocean exploration and conservation. Clark's greatest love was sharks. She once rode on the back of a 50-foot (15-m) whale shark. She called it one of the most exciting journeys of her life.

Earle poses with the suit she used to explore the ocean floor.

submersible wearing a pressurized suit. She explored the area. In the 1980s, Earle cofounded Deep Ocean Engineering Inc. This company makes underwater robots and vehicles. Earle has also worked with Japanese scientists to take submersibles 36,000 feet (10,973 m) below the surface of the sea.

Now Earle works at the National Geographic Society. She explores parts of the ocean that may be made into protected areas. Her 2014 film *Mission Blue* describes how oceans have changed over her lifetime. The film helps people understand the importance of protecting the sea. Ocean exploration runs in Earle's family. Her daughter, Liz Taylor, runs a company that builds remotely operated vehicles (ROVs). These machines explore the seas while human pilots control them from the surface.

IN THE REAL WORLD

Tara Willis, Undersea ROV Pilot

Tara Willis has always been fascinated with machines. In college she built an ROV to explore the oceans. Now she works with famed underwater explorer Dr. Robert Ballard. She is an ROV pilot on the underwater vehicle *Nautilus*. The *Nautilus* takes scientists down to study the ocean floor. ROVs attached to *Nautilus* help it carry out wide-ranging explorations.

Exploring the Deep

Dr. Cindy Lee Van Dover was the first woman to pilot the *Alvin*, a deep-ocean submersible vehicle. The *Alvin* carries a pilot and two scientists. From the *Alvin*, scientists take photos and samples of life on the ocean floor. Learning to pilot the submersible was not easy. Van Dover had to learn everything about how a submarine works. Some people wanted her to fail because she was a woman. Some even told her she shouldn't be a pilot. But Van Dover was determined. She became a successful pilot, leading 48 dives.

Van Dover studies deep-sea vent communities. These ecosystems are heated by volcanic activity on the ocean floor. They have unusual life forms, including six-foot (2-m) red tubeworms. Van Dover says, "When you're down there, you really see how this environment could have been the cradle of life on Earth."

Oceans cover 71 percent of Earth's surface. They contain 97 percent of the planet's water. Because

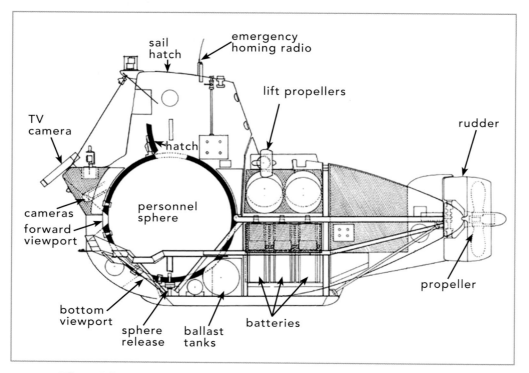

The *Alvin*

This diagram shows the many parts that make up the *Alvin*. Where do the scientists and pilot sit? Why might the crew's area make up such a small part of the ship? What dangers do submersible designers need to think about when building deep-sea exploration vessels?

of their great depth, approximately 95 percent of the ocean remains unexplored. The unknown areas represent an exciting opportunity for ocean explorers.

In a 2009 talk, Sylvia Earle discussed the many ways in which oceans have an impact on the environment:

> With every drop of water you drink, every breath you take, you're connected to the sea. No matter where on Earth you live. Most of the oxygen in the atmosphere is generated by the sea. Over time, most of the planet's organic carbon has been absorbed and stored there, mostly by microbes. The ocean drives climate and weather, stabilizes temperature, shapes Earth's chemistry. Water from the sea forms clouds that return to the land and the seas as rain, sleet, and snow, and provides home for about 97 percent of life in the world, maybe in the universe. No water, no life; no blue, no green. . . . Yet we have this idea, we humans, that the Earth—all of it: the oceans, the skies—are so vast and so resilient it doesn't matter what we do to it.

Source: Sylvia Earle. "My Wish: Protect Our Oceans." TED. TED, February 2009. Web. Accessed October 27, 2015.

Changing Minds

In this passage, Sylvia Earle describes why oceans are important. Take a position on the importance of protecting the oceans. Imagine your best friend has the opposite opinion. Write a short essay trying to change your friend's mind. Include facts to support your reasoning.

CHAPTER FOUR

WOMEN SAVING THE TROPICS

The tropics are the areas of Earth near the planet's equator. They cover vast areas of Africa, Asia, the Pacific Islands, and South America. They also cover Central America and the Caribbean. The world's largest rain forests are found within the tropics.

The tropics also include areas with plains, or savannas. Rain forests and savannas give us food, medicine, timber, and many other products.

The world's rain forests, including the Amazon of South America, are vulnerable to environmental damage.

IN THE REAL WORLD

Pacha Lotango, Female Eco-Guard

Pacha Lotango graduated at the top of her eco-guard class in the Democratic Republic of the Congo (DRC), a country in Africa. Eco-guards defend animals in conservation areas from poachers, or illegal hunters. In November 2014, an entire village attacked Lotango's team of eco-guards. Her team had arrested one of the villagers for poaching. Lotango was hit in the head and seriously injured. She took months to recover. Though Lotango could find a safer career, she chooses to do this dangerous but important job.

However, rain forests are being destroyed by logging, agriculture, and fire. Overgrazing by farm animals is turning savannas into deserts. Female conservationists have taken steps to protect these ecosystems.

Wangari Maathai

Wangari Maathai was born in Kenya in 1940. She worked for democracy, human rights, and environmental conservation. Her work was difficult because she was a woman. Kenya's president wanted Maathai to follow tradition and

Maathai won the Nobel Peace Prize in 2004. She was the first African woman to win the prize.

keep quiet. When she continued her work, she was jailed, beaten, and threatened.

Maathai is best known for starting the Green Belt Movement (GBM). The GBM pays women to plant trees. Trees prevent erosion, store rainwater, and provide both food and firewood to local families. By 2014 the GBM had planted 51 million trees.

Women Saving the Rain Forests

South America's Amazon is the world's largest rain forest. From the 1970s through the mid-2000s, it was rapidly logged. Pastures, farms, roads, mines, dams, and towns replaced trees. Deforestation has decreased since 2004. But the rain forests are still in danger. Conservationists are working to save them.

With her husband, Liliana Madrigal founded the Amazon Conservation Team (ACT). ACT partners with local people throughout the Amazon. They set up long-term projects to help manage the forest. They listen to elders who understand

Saving Biodiversity

Julie Hanta Razafimanahaka lives in Madagascar. This is an island country off the coast of Africa. She became interested in conservation when she was 13. She now directs a nonprofit organization that works to conserve biodiversity. She urges women to go into conservation. "The challenges that young women sometimes meet in the conservation field can be frightening, but we need to overcome this fear and move forward," she says.

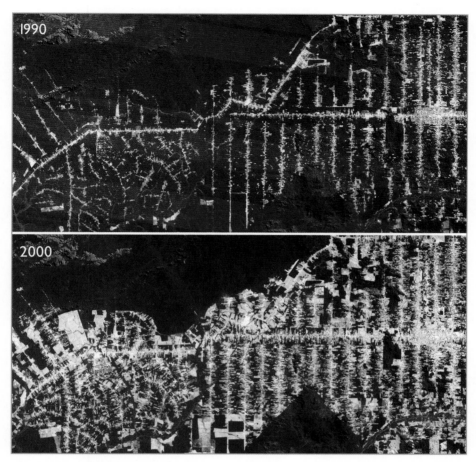

Amazon Deforestation

These satellite photos show a small section of the Amazon rain forest. The top image shows a part of the forest in 1990. The bottom image shows the same area in the year 2000. New roads and pathways were built for the logging workers. Areas cleared of trees are shown in white. What benefits do trees have to the environment? What negative effects might the removal of so many trees have?

the forest. Then they use this knowledge to improve the environment.

CHAPTER FIVE

THE FUTURE FOR WOMEN IN CONSERVATION

Today's key environmental problems include climate change, pollution, and overpopulation. These issues affect both people and habitats. Around the world, girls and women are stepping up to help. Many are trying to find ways to preserve wildlife while keeping people safe and healthy.

Even something as simple as planting trees can help the environment.

People and Wildlife Living Together

Elisabeth Kruger manages conflicts between polar bears and people. Kruger works for the World Wildlife Fund. Her home base is Alaska, but she also works in Canada and Russia. Polar bears do not recognize borders, so conservationists from these nations must cooperate.

Polar bears hunt on Arctic ice. As climate change causes the ice to melt, polar bears often cannot find food. They enter villages, lured by the smell of garbage. Conservationists learn from native people who have experience with the bears. Kruger is using this knowledge to protect both polar bears and people.

Dr. Krithi Karanth is another member of this new generation of conservationists. She understands that most people can no longer study animals in the creatures' natural habitats, as Jane Goodall did. In Karanth's home country of India, most natural habitats

Scientists estimate there are approximately 3,200 tigers left in the wild today.

are gone. India has more than 1 billion people. Only 3 percent of its land remains undeveloped. People are pushing tigers and Asian elephants out of their habitats. The animals then destroy people's crops. They may even attack people. Karanth wants to help people and animals live together.

Karanth conducts surveys and makes maps. She studies the border around the Kanha Tiger Reserve. This reserve protects Bengal tigers, wild dogs, leopards, and many other animals. People live and farm in the surrounding area. Many of them have

The Marvelous Maya Nut

Erika Vohman is working to bring back the Maya nut. This healthy nut was a common food in the past. Today, few people know about it. Vohman travels around Central America. She teaches women how to find, store, and prepare Maya nuts. The nuts can be used to make pancakes, cookies, salads, and soups. This helps very poor families who are short on food. It helps women gain skills and produce income. It also helps conserve the rain forest. Maya nuts are common, and harvesting them does not require clearing trees.

conflicts with wildlife. Animals sometimes eat their livestock or crops. Karanth finds peaceful solutions so that people and wildlife can live together. She says, "It is my generation's responsibility that we act now using the best science and link it to constructive, on-ground conservation action."

People Living in Natural Habitats

The Amazon's Sani Isla community is a strong voice for Amazon rain forest conservation. It is located between two protected areas in Ecuador. The women make traditional crafts to sell to tourists. This helps them learn business skills. It also allows them to provide their families with food and medicine. They have pledged to use their profits to fund education for girls.

Similar projects are occurring in Malaysia. One group of women has formed a fruit tree conservation project. They learn methods for pickling local mangoes. The village men pick the mangoes. The women

Women Changing Conservation

Environmental damage strongly affects women, especially in rural areas where they are often the ones collecting food and water. They are fighting back by becoming conservation leaders. To make sure women have a strong voice in conservation decisions, people and governments are working to:

- give women decision-making powers at local, national, and international levels;
- invest money to support women starting environmentally sound businesses; and
- invest money in STEM education for girls and women.

Across the world, many tourists flock to conservation sites to see wildlife.

pickle them. These practices increase their income while conserving trees. Another Malaysian group developed an ecotourism project. They found ways to open their village to tourists, who bring in income. Tourism provides good reasons for preserving the area's biodiversity.

American girls and women have much more freedom than those in many parts of the world. Still, women around the world are taking on leadership roles in the environmental movement. The head of an environmental agency in the United Arab Emirates is a woman, Razan Al Mubarak. She is proud that 50 percent of her agency's managers are women. She says, "Across gender . . . the environmental movement needs to be adopted by all of us, because it influences all of us." This is true for girls and women everywhere, whether they live in Asia, Europe, Africa, Australia, or the Americas.

FURTHER EVIDENCE

Review the chapter and determine its main point. List several facts that support the main point. Then read the news story at the website below. Find a quote from the story that supports the chapter's main point. Does the story add new information to your understanding of conservation?

Women as Environmental Change Agents
mycorelibrary.com/women-in-conservation

Think Globally, Act Locally

Some environmental problems are global. They affect the entire Earth. Climate change is a good example. But many problems begin locally and must be tackled locally. Think about your own community. Is there a polluted stream or lake? Is there a park or beach filled with litter that needs to be cleaned up? Is there a vacant lot that you could turn into a community garden? Choose a problem to solve.

You can work alone or with friends and fellow students. Get the support of your teachers and parents. Research the problem and decide how you can help. Make a plan and set a date. Then, do it! If it is a long-term project, such as a garden, be willing to see it through.

Become a Field Scientist

Choose an animal you want to understand better. It might be a pet dog or cat. It might be a bird, insect, raccoon, or other wild animal. It might be a zoo animal.

Put together a field research kit. You will need a pen and notebook (or a computer) to take notes. A camera and

a pair of binoculars would also be helpful. Dress properly for the environment where your animal lives.

Watch the animal. Take notes on everything it does. You might have specific questions you want to answer. You might wonder what the animal eats, how it greets other animals of the same kind, and so on. Observe carefully. Look for unusual behaviors. Above all, be patient. Field scientists watch animals for days, months, or even years.

Why Do I Care?

Some of the animals mentioned in the book, such as polar bears and sea turtles, may live a long way from where you are. But conservation issues affect everyone on the planet. Research a conservation issue near where you live. It may be an endangered species, a polluted area, or a threatened habitat. Write a paragraph about the issue and how it might affect you or someone you know.

Surprise Me

Chapter Three discusses the work of ocean conservationists Sylvia Earle and Cindy Lee Van Dover. After reading this book, what two or three facts about their work did you find most surprising? Write a few sentences about each fact. Why did you find each fact surprising?

Take a Stand

This book discusses how Jane Goodall's research methods differed from the accepted scientific studies of her time. Do you agree with how she did her work? Or do you believe she should have followed the usual scientific process used by others? Why?

Tell the Tale

Chapter Five discusses women who help their communities economically while also protecting the environment. Imagine you are living with one of these groups. What is your day like? What kinds of things do you see? How do you help them achieve their goals?

GLOSSARY

activist
a person who works for change in society, for example, an environmental activist or a social activist

ethology
the scientific study of animal behavior

pesticide
a substance used to kill insects or other pests

biodiversity
the variety of living things; the number of different kinds of organisms

poacher
person who trespasses on private or conserved land to hunt or fish illegally

ecosystem
a natural system including all living organisms and nonliving factors in an area, plus the interactions occurring in this system

submersible
an underwater vehicle, usually designed for deep ocean research and exploration

LEARN MORE

Books

Gagne, Tammy. *Rain Forest Ecosystems.* Minneapolis, MN: Abdo Publishing, 2016.

Rowell, Rebecca. *Rachel Carson Sparks the Environmental Movement.* Minneapolis, MN: Abdo Publishing, 2016.

Sepahban, Lois. *Jane Goodall: Revolutionary Primatologist and Anthropologist.* Minneapolis, MN: Abdo Publishing, 2016.

Websites

To learn more about Women in STEM, visit **booklinks.abdopublishing.com**. These links are routinely monitored and updated to provide the most current information available.

Visit **mycorelibrary.com** for free additional tools for teachers and students.

INDEX

ABOUT THE AUTHOR

Carol Hand has a PhD in zoology with a special interest in environmental problems. She has written more than 30 books on topics including the possibility of extraterrestrial life, environmental engineering, and careers for girls in technology.